The Royal Horticultural Society

TREASURY *of*
GARDEN VERSE

The Royal Horticultural Society

TREASURY *of* GARDEN VERSE

With illustrations from the
Royal Horticultural Society's Lindley Library

FRANCES LINCOLN

Frances Lincoln Limited
4 Torriano Mews
Torriano Avenue
London NW5 2RZ
www.franceslincoln.com

The Royal Horticultural Society Treasury of Garden Verse
Copyright © Frances Lincoln Limited 2003

Illustrations copyright © The Royal Horticultural Society 2003
and printed under licence granted by the Royal Horticultural Society,
Registered Charity number 222879.
www.rhs.org.uk

The Publishers would like to extend their thanks to Brian Shawcross for
all his help in selecting the poems and to Susanne Mitchell for her advice
and support.

British Library cataloguing-in-publication data
A catalogue record for this book is available from the British Library

ISBN 0-7112-2073-5

Printed and bound in China by Kwong Fat Offset Printing Co. Ltd
First Frances Lincoln edition 2003

CONTENTS

SEASONS

To Every Thing there is a Season

To every thing there is a season,
    and a time to every purpose under the heaven:
A time to be born, and a time to die; a time to plant,
    and a time to pluck up that which is planted;
A time to kill, and a time to heal; a time to break down,
    and a time to build up;
A time to weep, and a time to laugh; a time to mourn,
    and a time to dance;
A time to cast away stones, and a time to gather
    stones together; a time to embrace,
    and a time to refrain from embracing;
A time to get, and a time to lose; a time to keep,
    and a time to cast away;
A time to rend, and a time to sew; a time to keep silence,
    and a time to speak;
A time to love, and a time to hate; a time of war,
    and a time of peace.

From Ecclesiastes, *Chapter 3*

THE MONTHS

January brings the snow,
Makes our feet and fingers glow.

February brings the rain,
Thaws the frozen lake again.

March brings breezes loud and shrill,
Stirs the dancing daffodil.

April brings the primrose sweet,
Scatters daisies at our feet.

May brings flocks of pretty lambs,
Skipping by their fleecy dams.

June brings tulips, lilies, roses,
Fills the children's hands with posies.

Hot July brings cooling showers,
Apricots and gillyflowers.

August brings the sheaves of corn,
Then the harvest home is borne.

Warm September brings the fruit,
Sportsmen then begin to shoot.

Fresh October brings the pheasant,
Then to gather nuts is pleasant.

Dull November brings the blast,
Then the leaves are whirling fast.

Chill December brings the sleet,
Blazing fire, and Christmas treat.

Sara Coleridge (1802–52)

HOME THOUGHTS FROM ABROAD

Oh, to be in England
Now that April's there,
And whoever wakes in England
Sees, some morning, unaware,
That the lowest boughs and the brushwood sheaf
Round the elm-tree bole are in tiny leaf.
While the chaffinch sings on the orchard bough
In England – now!

And after April, when May follows,
And the whitethroat builds, and all the swallows!
Hark, where my blossomed pear-tree in the hedge
Leans to the field and scatters on the clover
Blossoms and dewdrops – at the bent spray's edge –
That's the wise thrush; he sings each song twice over,
Lest you should think he never could recapture
The first fine careless rapture!
And though the fields look rough with hoary dew,
All will be gay when noontide wakes anew
The buttercups, the little children's dower
– Far brighter than this gaudy melon-flower!

Robert Browning (1812–89)

APRIL

April's the busy month, the month that grows
Faster than hand can follow at its task;
No time to relish and no time to bask,
(Though when indeed is that the gardener's lot,
However large, however small his plot?)
April's the month for pruning of the rose,
April's the month when the good gardener sows
More annuals for summer, cheap and quick,
Yet always sows too thick
From penny packets scattered on a patch
With here a batch of poppy, there a batch
Of the low candytuft or scabious tall
That country children call
Pincushions, with their gift
Of accurate observance and their swift
Naming more vivid than the botanist.
So the good gardener will sow his drift
Of larkspur and forget-me-not
To fill blank space, or recklessly to pick;
And gay nasturtium writhing up a fence
Splotching with mock of sunlight sunless days
When latening summer brings the usual mist.

He is a millionaire for a few pence.
Squandering Nature in her gift exceeds
Even her own demands.

Consider not the lily, but her seeds
In membrane tissue packed within the pod
With skill that fools the skill of human hands;
The poppy with her cracking pepper-pot
That spills in ripened moment split asunder;
The foxglove with her shower fine as snuff.
Consider these with thankfulness and wonder,
Nor ever ask why that same God
If it was He who made the flow'rs, made weeds:

The thistle and the groundsel with their fluff;
The little cresses that in waste explode
Mistaken bounty at the slightest touch;
The couch-grass throwing roots at every node,
With wicked nick-names like its wicked self,
Twitch, quitch, quack, scutch;
The gothic teazle, tall as hollyhock,
Heraldic as a halberd and as tough;
The romping bindweed and the rooting dock;
The sheeny celandine that Wordsworth praised,
(He was no gardener, his eyes were raised;)
The dandelion, cheerful children's clock
Making a joke of minutes and of hours,
Ironical to us who wryly watch;
Oh why, we ask, reversing good intentions,
Was Nature so ingenious in inventions,
And why did He who must make weeds, make flowers?

from The Garden
Vita Sackville-West (1892–1962)

COME – GONE

Gone the snowdrop – comes the crocus;
With the tulip blows the squill;
Jonquil white as wax between them,
And the nid-nod daffodil.

Peach, plum, cherry, pear and apple,
Rain-sweet lilac on the spray;
Come the dog-rose in the hedges –
Gone's the sweetness of the may.

Walter de la Mare (1873–1956)

DRINKING

The thirsty earth soaks up the rain,
And drinks and gapes for drink again;
The plants suck in the earth, and are
With constant drinking fresh and fair;
The sea itself (which one would think
Should have but little need of drink)
Drinks ten thousand rivers up,
So filled that they o'erflow the cup.
The busy Sun (and one would guess
By 's drunken fiery face no less)
Drinks up the sea, and when he's done,
The Moon and Stars drink up the sun:
They drink and dance by their own light,
They drink and revel all the night:
Nothing in Nature's sober found,
But an eternal health goes round.
Fill up the bowl, then, fill it high,
Fill all the glasses there – for why
Should every creature drink but I?
Why, man of morals, tell me why?

Abraham Cowley (1618–67)

A CONTEMPLATION UPON FLOWERS

Brave flowers – that I could gallant it like you,
    And be as little vain!
You come abroad, and make a harmless show,
    And to your beds of earth again.
You are not proud: you know your birth:
For your embroider'd garments are from earth.

You do obey your months and times, but I
    Would have it ever Spring:
My fate would know no Winter, never die,
    Nor think of such a thing.
O that I could my bed of earth but view
And smile, and look as cheerfully as you!

O teach me to see Death and not to fear,
    But rather to take truce!
How often have I seen you at a bier,
    And there look fresh and spruce!
You fragrant flowers! then teach me, that my breath
Like yours may sweeten and perfume my death.

Henry King, Bishop of Chichester (1592–1669)

Groote Nooten.   *Hafe Nooten.*

To Autumn

Season of mists and mellow fruitfulness!
　Close bosom-friend of the maturing sun;
Conspiring with him how to load and bless
　With fruit the vines that round the thatch-eaves run;
To bend with apples the mossed cottage-trees,
　And fill all fruit with ripeness to the core;
　　To swell the gourd, and plump the hazel shells
With a sweet kernel; to set budding more,
　And still more, later flowers for the bees,
　Until they think warm days will never cease,
　　For Summer has o'erbrimmed their clammy cells.

Who hath not seen thee oft amid thy store?
　Sometimes whoever seeks abroad may find
Thee sitting careless on a granary floor,
　Thy hair soft-lifted by the winnowing wind,
Or on a half-reaped furrow sound asleep,
　Drowsed with the fume of poppies, while thy hook
　　Spares the next swath and all its twinèd flowers;
And sometimes like a gleaner thou dost keep
　Steady thy laden head across a brook;
　Or by a cider-press, with patient look,
　　Thou watchest the last oozings hours by hours.

Where are the songs of Spring? Ay, where are they?
　Think not of them, thou hast thy music too, –
While barred clouds bloom the soft-dying day,

And touch the stubble-plains with rosy hue;
Then in a wailful choir the small gnats mourn
Among the river sallows, borne aloft
    Or sinking as the light wind lives or dies;
And full-grown lambs loud bleat from hilly bourn;
    Hedge-crickets sing; and now with treble soft
    The redbreast whistles from a garden-croft;
        And gathering swallows twitter in the skies.

John Keats (1795–1821)

AUTUMN

I love the fitful gust that shakes
    The casement all the day,
And from the glossy elm-tree takes
    The faded leaves away,
Twirling them by the window-pane
With thousand others down the lane.

I love to see the shaking twig
    Dance till shut of eve,
The sparrow on the cottage rig,
    Whose chirp would make believe
That Spring was just now flirting by
In Summer's lap with flowers to lie.

I love to see the cottage smoke
    Curl upwards through the trees,
The pigeons nestled round the cote
    On November days like these;
The cock upon the dunghill crowing,
The mill-sails on the heath a-going.

The feather from the raven's breast
    Falls on the stubble lea;
The acorns near the old crow's nest
    Fall pattering down the tree;
The grunting pigs, that wait for all,
Scramble and hurry where they fall.

John Clare (1793–1864)

FAIR IS THE WORLD

Fair is the world, now autumn's wearing,
And the sluggard sun lies long abed;
Sweet are the days, now winter's nearing,
And all winds feign that the wind is dead.

Dumb is the hedge where the crabs hang yellow,
Bright as the blossoms of the spring;
Dumb is the close where the pears grow mellow,
And none but the dauntless redbreasts sing.

Fair was the spring, but amidst his greening
Grey were the days of the hidden sun;
Fair was the summer, but overweening,
So soon his o'er-sweet days were done.

Come then, love, for peace is upon us,
Far off is failing, and far is fear,
Here where the rest in the end hath won us,
In the garnering tide of the happy year.

Come from the grey old house by the water,
Where, far from the lips of the hungry sea,
Green groweth the grass o'er the field of the slaughter,
And all is a tale for thee and me.

from The Story of the Glittering Plain
William Morris (1834–96)

GARDENING

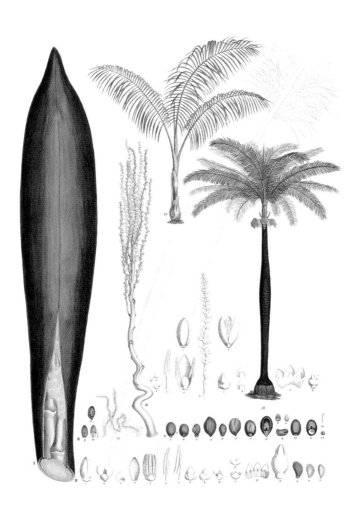

PALM TREE KING

Because I come from the West Indies
certain people in England seem to think
I is a expert on palm trees

So not wanting to sever dis link
with me native roots (know what ah mean?)
or to disappoint dese culture vulture
I does smile cool as seabreeze

and say to dem
which specimen
you interested in
cause you talking
to the right man
I is palm tree king
I know palm tree history
like de palm o me hand
In fact me navel string
bury under a palm tree

If you think de queen could wave
you ain't see nothing yet
till you see the Roystonea Regia
– that is the royal palm –

with she crown of leaves
waving calm–calm
over the blue Caribbean carpet
nearly 100 feet of royal highness

But let we get down to business
Tell me what you want to know
How tall a palm tree does grow?
What is the biggest coconut I ever see?
What is the average length of the leaf?

Don't expect me to be brief
cause palm tree history
is a long–long story

Anyway why you so interested
in length and circumference?
That kind of talk so ordinary
That don't touch the essence
of palm tree mystery
That is no challenge
to a palm tree historian like me

Is you insist on statistics
why you don't pose a question
with some mathematical profundity?

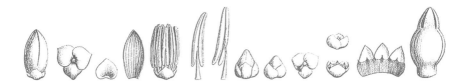

Ask me something more tricky
like if a American tourist with a camera
take 9 minutes to climb a coconut tree
how long a English tourist without a camera
would take to climb the same coconut tree?

That is problem pardner
Now ah coming harder

If 6 straw hat
and half a dozen bikini
multiply by the same number of coconut tree
equal one postcard
how many square miles of straw hat
you need to make a tourist industry?

That is problem pardner
Find the solution
and you got a revolution

But before you say anything
let I palm tree king
give you dis warning
Ah want de answer in metric
it kind of rhyme with tropic
Besides it sound more exotic

John Agard (1949–)

CAPABILITY BROWN

Lo, he comes!
Th' omnipotent magician, Brown, appears!
Down falls the venerable pile, th' abode
Of our forefathers – a grave whisker'd race,
But tasteless. Springs a palace in its stead,
But in a distant spot; where, more expos'd,
It may enjoy th' advantage of the north,
And aguish east, till time shall have transform'd
Those naked acres to a shelt'ring grove.
He speaks. The lake in front becomes a lawn;
Woods vanish, hills subside, and valleys rise:
And streams, as if created for his use,
Pursue the track of his directing wand,
Sinuous or straight, now rapid and now slow,
Now murm'ring soft, now roaring in cascades –
Ev'n as he bids! Th' enraptured owner smiles.
'Tis finish'd, and yet, finish'd as it seems,
Still wants a grace, the loveliest it could show,
A mine to satisfy th' enormous cost.
Drain'd to the last poor item of his wealth,
He sighs, departs, and leaves th' accomplished plan
That he has touch'd, retouch'd, many a long day
Labour'd, and many a night pursu'd in dreams,
Just when it meets his hopes, and proves the heav'n
He wanted, for a wealthier to enjoy!

from The Task
William Cowper (1731–1800)

INSCRIPTION ON THE PALM HOUSE DOORS, BICTON HOUSE, EAST BUDLEIGH, DEVON, *c.* 1850

The Gardener at a hole looks out
And holes are plenty hereabout
A pair of pistols by his lug
One load with ball the other slug
A blunderbus of cannon shape
Just ready to discharge with grape
Let midnight thief or robber stand
And pause ere he puts out his hand
While those who come in open day
May look but carry nought away.

A FRAGMENT OF TRUTH

While working in the garden recently, I dug up
   a small fragment of truth.

It was adherent all over with clay, and must have been
   buried for many years, but I recognised what it was
   almost at once.

At first we kept it on the mantelpiece in the living room,
   but it was often embarrassing to visitors and I eventually
   put it on my desk in the study, for a paper-weight.

I asked several close friends what they thought I ought to do
   with it, but no one was sure. 'Keep it for your children,'
   some said, 'It is a great curiosity.' Others suggested
   the local museum.

It was too heavy to take with us when we went on our holidays.
   While we were gone, someone broke into the house and stole it.
   The police said that they would make investigations,
   and asked me, 'Could you identify it again as yours, if you
   saw it?'

Perhaps. But I'm not sure if I do want it back. After all,
   if whoever it was should have found some use for it. . .

Gael Turnbull (1928–)

MY NEIGHBOR'S ROSES

The roses red upon my neighbor's vine
Are owned by him, but they are also mine.
His was the cost, and his the labor, too,
But mine as well as his the joy, their loveliness to view.

They bloom for me and are for me as fair
As for the man who gives them all his care.
Thus I am rich, because a good man grew
A rose-clad vine for all his neighbors' view.

I know from this that others plant for me,
And what they own, my joy may also be.
So why be selfish, when so much that's fine
Is grown for you, upon your neighbor's vine.

Abraham L. Gruber (1807–82)

PLANTS

WHAT IS PINK?

What is pink? A rose is pink
By the fountain's brink.
What is red? A poppy's red
In its barley bed.
What is blue? The sky is blue
Where the clouds float through.
What is white? A swan is white
Sailing in the light.
What is yellow? Pears are yellow,
Rich and ripe and mellow.
What is green? The grass is green
With small flowers between.
What is violet? Clouds are violet
In the summer twilight.
What is orange? Why, an orange,
Just an orange!

Christina Rossetti (1830–94)

TREES

I think that I shall never see
A poem lovely as a tree.

A tree whose hungry mouth is pressed
Against the earth's sweet flowing breast;

A tree that looks at God all day,
And lifts her leafy arms to pray;

A tree that may in summer wear
A nest of robins in her hair;

Upon whose bosom snow has lain;
Who intimately lives with rain.

Poems are made by fools like me,
But only God can make a tree.

Joyce Kilmer (1886–1918)

OPHELIA'S FLOWERS

There's rosemary, that's for remembrance;
    pray you, love, remember.
And there is pansies, that's for thoughts.
    . . . There's fennel for you,
and columbines. There's rue for you; and here's some for me.
We may call it herb of grace o' Sundays:
    O! you may wear your rue
with a difference. There's a daisy:
    I would give you some violets,
but they withered all when my father died.
    They say he made a good end . . .

from Hamlet, *Act 4, Scene 5*
William Shakespeare (1564–1616)

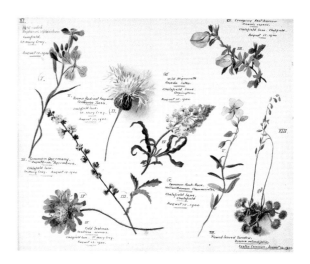

FIELD PATH

The beans in blossom with their spots of jet
Smelt sweet as gardens wheresoever met;
The level meadow grass was in the swath;
The hedge briar rose hung right across the path,
White over with its flowers – the grass that lay
Bleaching beneath the twittering heat to hay
Smelt so deliciously, the puzzled bee
Went wondering where the honeyed sweets could be;
And passer-by along the level rows
Stooped down and whipt a bit beneath his nose.

John Clare (1793–1864)

MUSHROOMS

Overnight, very
Whitely, discreetly,
Very quietly

Our toes, our noses
Take hold on the loam,
Acquire the air.

Nobody sees us,
Stops us, betrays us;
The small grains make room.

Soft fists insist on
Heaving the needles,
The leafy bedding,

Even the paving,
Our hammers, our rams,
Earless and eyeless,

Perfectly voiceless,
Widen the crannies,
Shoulder through holes. We

Diet on water,
On crumbs of shadow,
Bland-mannered, asking

Little or nothing.
So many of us!
So many of us!

We are shelves, we are
Tables, we are meek,
We are edible,

Nudgers and shovers
In spite of ourselves.
Our kind multiplies:

We shall by morning
Inherit the earth.
Our foot's in the door.

Sylvia Plath (1932–63)

ONE PERFECT ROSE

A single flow'r he sent me, since we met.
　　All tenderly his messenger he chose;
Deep-hearted, pure, with scented dew still wet –
　　One perfect rose.

I knew the language of the floweret;
　　'My fragile leaves', it said, 'his heart enclose.'
Love long has taken for his amulet
　　One perfect rose.

Why is it no one ever sent me yet
　　One perfect limousine, do you suppose?
Ah no, it's always just my luck to get
　　One perfect rose.

Dorothy Parker (1893–1967)

HOW LILLIES CAME WHITE

White though ye be; yet, Lillies, know,
From the first ye were not so:
   But Ilel tell ye
   What befell ye;
Cupid and his Mother lay
In a Cloud; while both did play,
He with his pretty fingers prest
The rubie niplet of her breast;
Out of which, the creame of light,
   Like to a Dew,
   Fell downe on you
   And made ye white.

Robert Herrick (1591–1674)

THE DAISY

The daisy is a happy flower,
    And comes at early spring,
And brings with it the sunny hour
    When bees are on the wing.

It brings with it the butterfly,
    And early humble-bee;
With the polyanthus' golden eye,
    And blooming apple-tree;

Hedge-sparrows from the mossy nest
    In the old garden hedge,
Where schoolboys, in their idle glee,
    Seek pooties as their pledge.

The cow stands browsing all the day
    Over the orchard gate,
And eats her bit of sweet old hay;
    And Goody stands to wait,

Lest what's not eaten the rude wind
    May rise and snatch away
Over the neighbour's hedge behind,
    Where hungry cattle lay.

John Clare (1793–1864)

AH! SUN-FLOWER!

Ah, Sun-flower! weary of time,
Who countest the steps of the Sun:
Seeking after that sweet golden clime,
Where the traveller's journey is done.

Where the Youth pined away with desire,
And the pale Virgin shrouded in snow
Arise from their graves and aspire,
Where my Sun-flower wishes to go.

William Blake (1757–1827)

To Daffodils

Fair daffodils, we weep to see
   You haste away so soon;
As yet the early-rising sun
   Has not attained his noon.
     Stay, stay
   Until the hasting day
     Has run
   But to the evensong;
And, having prayed together, we
   Will go with you along.

We have short time to stay as you,
   We have as short a spring;
As quick a growth to meet decay,
   As you, or anything.
     We die
   As your hours do, and dry
     Away
   Like to the summer's rain;
Or as the pearls of morning's dew,
   Ne'er to be found again.

Robert Herrick (1591–1674)

"Southover". Burwash
Sussex.

THE LAST ROSE OF SUMMER

'Tis the last rose of summer left blooming alone,
All her lovely companions are faded and gone.
No flower of her kindred, no rosebud is nigh
To reflect back her blushes or give sigh for sigh.

I'll not leave thee, thou lone one, to pine on the stem;
Since the lovely are sleeping, go sleep thou with them:
Thus kindly I scatter thy leaves o'er the bed
Where thy mates of the garden lie scentless and dead.

So soon may I follow when friendships decay,
And from love's shining circle the gems drop away.
When true hearts lie withered and fond ones are flown,
Oh who would inhabit this bleak world alone?

Thomas Moore (1779–1852)

I SOMETIMES THINK ...

I sometimes think that never blows so red
The rose as where some buried Caesar bled;
  That every hyacinth the garden wears
Dropped in her lap from some once lovely head.

And this reviving herb whose tender green
Fledges the river-lip on which we lean –
  Ah, lean upon it lightly! for who knows
From what once lovely lip it springs unseen!

from The Rubáiyát of Omar Khayyám
Edward FitzGerald (1809–83)

MARIGOLDS

Not the flowers men give women –
delicately-scented freesias,
stiff red roses, carnations
the shades of bridesmaids' dresses,
almost sapless flowers,
drying and fading – but flowers
that wilt as soon as their stems
are cut, leaves blackening
as if blighted by the enzymes
in our breath, rotting to a slime
we have to scour from the rims
of vases; flowers that burst
from tight, explosive buds, rayed
like the sun, that lit the path
up the Thracian mountain, that we wound
into our hair, stamped on
in ecstatic dance, that remind us
we are killers, can tear the heads
off men's shoulders;
flowers we still bring
secretly and shamefully
into the house, stroking
our arms and breasts and legs
with their hot orange fringes,
the smell of arousal.

Vicki Feaver (1943–)

RED GERANIUM AND GODLY MIGNONETTE

Imagine that any mind ever *thought* a red geranium!
As if the redness of a red geranium could be anything
   but a sensual experience
and as if sensual experience could take place
   before there were any senses.
We know that even God could not imagine
   the redness of a red geranium
nor the smell of mignonette
when geraniums were not, and mignonette neither.
And even when they were,
   even God would have to have a nose
to smell at the mignonette.
You can't imagine the Holy Ghost sniffing
   at cherry-pie heliotrope.
Or the Most High, during the coal age,
   cudgelling his mighty brains
even if he had any brains: straining his mighty mind
to think, among the moss and mud of lizards
   and mastodons
to think out, in the abstract,
   when all was twilit green and muddy:
'Now there shall be tum-tiddly-um, and tum-tiddly-um,
hey-presto! scarlet geranium!'
We know it couldn't be done.
But imagine, among the mud and the mastodons

God sighing and yearning with tremendous
    creative yearning, in that dark green mess
oh, for some other beauty, some other beauty
that blossomed at last, red geranium, and mignonette.

D.H. Lawrence (1885–1930)

CREATURES

The Caterpillar

Brown and furry
Caterpillar in a hurry,
Take your walk
To the shady leaf, or stalk,
Or what not,
Which may be the chosen spot.
No toad spy you,
Hovering bird of prey pass by you:
Spin and die,
To live again a butterfly.

Christina Rossetti (1830–94)

GREEN MAN IN THE GARDEN

Green man in the garden
    Staring from the tree,
Why do you look so long and hard
    Through the pane at me?

Your eyes are dark as holly,
    Of sycamores your horns,
Your bones are made of elder-branch,
    Your teeth are made of thorns.

Your hat is made of ivy-leaf,
    Of bark your dancing shoes,
And evergreen and green and green
    Your jacket and shirt and trews.

Leave your house and leave your land
    And throw away the key,
And never look behind, he creaked,
    And come and live with me.

I bolted up the window,
    I bolted up the door,
I drew the blind that I should find
    The green man never more.

But when I softly turned the stair
    As I went up to bed,
I saw the green man standing there,
    Sleep well, my friend, he said.

Charles Causley (1917–)

Jeremiah, the Tabby Cat,
Stalks in the Sunlit Garden

While you clamber over the blue gate in the garden,
In the sunlit garden I
Already arrived am before you: while
In a flash of the eye,
You are suspended in your leap
Against the blue ground of the gate. And then,
Unconscious cinema-actor, you cross your stage,
The plot where light cuts the shade like a jewel
On what intent?
Your eyes are amber in the sun, flashing
From the cushioned tuft of harebells
And calceolarias.
Now you thread the intricate pattern
Of garden stems and stems of shadow,
And cross the lawn:
Your supple flanks serpentine, your tread
Stealthy and secret, of who knows
What generations of jungle cats?
And so you reach the undergrowth of the sycamore;
Nor pause to hear me calling from my window
Whence sight of you I lose,
Your dappled side lost in the camouflage of shadow;
And you have left the sunlit garden
For who knows what memories of lost generations of
    great cats?

A.L. Rowse (1903–97)

BUGS

Some insects feed on rosebuds,
And others feed on carrion,
Between them they devour the earth,
Bugs are totalitarian.

Ogden Nash (1902–71)

Lady-bird! lady-bird! fly away home,
Night is approaching and sunset is come,
The herons are flown to their trees by the Hall,
Felt but unseen the damp dew-drops fall.
This is the close of a still summer day.
Lady-bird! lady-bird, haste, fly away.

Charlotte Brontë (1816–55)

Satyrion   Madelieven   Leucojon Triphyllo

The Connoisseuse of Slugs

When I was a connoisseuse of slugs
I would part the ivy leaves, and look for the
naked jelly of those gold bodies,
translucent strangers glistening along the
stones, slowly, their gelatinous bodies
at my mercy. Made mostly of water,
    they would shrivel
to nothing if they were sprinkled with salt,
but I was not interested in that. What I liked
was to draw aside the ivy, breathe the
odor of the wall, and stand there in silence
until the slug forgot I was there
and sent its antennae up out of its
head, the glimmering umber horns
rising like telescopes, until finally the
sensitive knobs would pop out the ends,
delicate and intimate. Years later,
when I first saw a naked man,
I gasped with pleasure to see that quiet
mystery reenacted, the slow
elegant being coming out of hiding and
gleaming in the dark air, eager and so
trusting you could weep.

       Sharon Olds (1942–)

Upon a Snail

She goes but softly, but she goeth sure;
She stumbles not, as stronger creatures do;
Her journey's shorter, so she may endure
Better than they which do much farther go.
She makes no noise, but stilly seizeth on
The flower or herb appointed for her food,
The which she quietly doth feed upon,
While others range and glare, but find no good.
And though she doth but very softly go,
However 'tis not fast, nor slow, but sure;
And certainly they that do travel so,
The prize they do aim at they do procure.

John Bunyan (1628–88)

ARIEL'S SONG

Where the bee sucks, there suck I,
In a cowslip's bell I lie;
There I couch when owls do cry.
On the bat's back I do fly
After summer merrily:
Merrily, merrily shall I live now
Under the blossom that hangs on the bough.

from The Tempest, *Act 5, Scene 1*
William Shakespeare (1564–1616)

FAIRIES

There are fairies at the bottom of our garden!
It's not so very, very far away;
You pass the gardener's shed and you just keep straight ahead –
I do so hope they've really come to stay.
There's a little wood, with moss in it and beetles,
And a little stream that quietly runs through;
You wouldn't think they'd dare to come merrymaking there –
    Well, they do.

There are fairies at the bottom of our garden!
They often have a dance on summer nights;
The butterflies and bees make a lovely little breeze,
And the rabbits stand about and hold the lights.
Did you know that they could sit upon the moonbeams
And pick a little star to make a fan,
And dance away up there in the middle of the air?
    Well, they can.

There are fairies at the bottom of our garden!
You cannot think how beautiful they are;
They all stand up and sing when the Fairy Queen and King
Come gently floating down upon their car.
The King is very proud and *very* handsome;
The Queen – now can you guess who that could be
(She's a little girl all day, but at night she steals away)?
    Well – it's *Me!*

Rose Fyleman (1877–1957)

GARDCHRON

GARDENS

My Garden

A garden is a lovesome thing, God wot!
    Rose plot,
    Fringed pool,
Ferned grot –
    The veriest school
    Of peace; and yet the fool
Contends that God is not –
Not God! in gardens! when the eve is cool?
    Nay, but I have a sign;
    'Tis very sure God walks in mine.

Thomas Edward Brown (1830–97)

CHERRY-RIPE

There is a garden in her face
    Where roses and white lilies blow;
A heavenly paradise is that place,
    Wherein all pleasant fruits do flow:
        There cherries grow which none may buy
        Till 'Cherry-ripe' themselves do cry.

Those cherries fairly do enclose
    Of orient pearls a double row,
Which when her lovely laughter shows,
    They look like rose-buds fill'd with snow;
        Yet them nor peer nor prince can buy
        Till 'Cherry-ripe' themselves do cry.

Her eyes like angels watch them still;
    Her brows like bended bows do stand,
Threat'ning with piercing frowns to kill
    All that attempt with eye or hand
        Those sacred cherries to come nigh,
        Till 'Cherry-ripe' themselves do cry.

Thomas Campion (1567–1620)

PARADISE

Thus was this place
A happy rural seat of various view;
Groves whose rich Trees wept odorous Gumms
    and Balme,
Others whose fruit, burnisht with Golden Rinde
Hung amiable, Hesperian Fables true,
If true, here only, and of delicious taste:
Betwixt them Lawns, or level Downs, and Flocks
Grasing the tender herb, were interpos'd,
Or palmy hilloc; or the flourie lap
Of some irriguous Valley spread her store,
Flow'rs of all hue, and without Thorn the Rose:
Another side, umbrageous Grots and Caves
Of coole recess, o're which the mantling Vine
Layes forth her purple Grape, and gently creeps
Luxuriant; mean while murmuring waters fall
Down the slope hills, disperst, or in a Lake,
That to the fringèd Bank with Myrtle crownd
Her chrystall mirror holds, unite thir streams.
The Birds thir quire apply; aires, vernal aires,
Breathing the smell of field and grove, attune
The trembling leaves, while Universal Pan
Knit with the Graces and the Hours in dance
Led on th' Eternal Spring.

from Paradise Lost, *Book 4*
John Milton (1608–74)

THE GARDEN

How vainly men themselves amaze
To win the Palm, the Oke, or Bayes;
And their uncessant Labours see
Crown'd from some single Herb or Tree,
Whose short and narrow-vergèd shade
Does prudently their Toyles upbraid;
While all Flow'rs and all Trees do close
To weave the Garlands of repose!

Fair Quiet, have I found thee here,
And Innocence, thy Sister dear?
Mistaken long, I sought you then
In busy Companies of Men:
Your sacred Plants, if here below,
Only among the Plants will grow:
Society is all but rude
To this delicious Solitude.

No white nor red was ever seen
So am'rous as this lovely green.
Fond Lovers, cruel as their Flame
Cut in these Trees their Mistress' name;
Little, alas! they know or heed
How far these Beauties Hers exceed!
Fair Trees! Wheresoe'er your barks I wound,
No Name shall but your own be found.

When we have run our Passions' heat,
Love hither makes his best retreat;
The Gods, that mortal Beauty chase,
Still in a tree did end their race;
Apollo hunted Daphne so,
Only that She might Laurel grow;
And Pan did after Syrinz speed,
Not as a Nymph, but for a Reed.

What wond'rous Life in this I lead!
Ripe Apples drop about my head;
The Luscious Clusters of the Vine
Upon my Mouth do crush their Wine;
The Nectaren, and curious Peach
Into my hands themselves do reach;
Stumbling on Melons, as I pass,
Insnar'd with Flow'rs, I fall on Grass.

Mean while the Mind from Pleasure less
Withdraws into its happiness;
The Mind, that Ocean where each kind
Does streight its own resemblance find;
Yet it creates, transcending these,
Far other Worlds, and other Seas;
Annihilating all that's made
To a green Thought in a green Shade.

Here at the Fountain's sliding foot,
Or at some Fruit-trees mossy root,
Casting the Bodies Vest aside,
My Soul into the bough does glide;
There, like a Bird it sits, and sings,
Then whets and combs its silver Wings,
And, till prepar'd for longer flight,
Waves in its Plumes the various Light.

Such was that happy Garden-state
While Man there walk'd without a Mate:
After a Place so pure and sweet,
What other Help could yet be meet!
But 'twas beyond a Mortal's share
To wander solitary there:
Two Paradises 'twere in one
To live in Paradise alone.

How well the skillful Gardner drew
Of flow'rs and herbes this Dial new
Where, from above, the milder Sun
Does through a fragrant Zodiac run;
And, as it works, th' industrious Bee
Computes its time as well as we.
How could such sweet and wholesome Hours
Be reckon'd, but with herbs and flow'rs!

Andrew Marvell (1621–78)

Magdalen Walks

The little white clouds are racing over the sky,
    And the fields are strewn with the gold of the flower
        of March,
    The daffodil breaks under foot, and the tasselled larch
Sways and swings as the thrush goes hurrying by.

A delicate odour is borne on the wings
      of the morning breeze,
    The odour of deep wet grass, and of brown
      new-furrowed earth,
    The birds are singing for joy of the Spring's glad birth,
Hopping from branch to branch on the rocking trees.

And all the woods are alive with the murmur
      and sound of spring,
    And the rose bud breaks into pink on the climbing briar,
    And the crocus-bed is a quivering moon of fire
Girdled round with the belt of an amethyst ring.

And the plane to the pine-tree is whispering some tale
      of love
    Till it rustles with laughter and tosses its mantle of green,
    And the gloom of the wych-elm's hollow is lit
      with the iris sheen
Of the burnished rainbow throat and the silver breast
      of a dove.

See! the lark starts up from his bed in the meadow there,
   Breaking the gossamer threads and the nets of dew,
   And flashing adown the river, a flame of blue!
The kingfisher flies like an arrow, and wounds the air.

And the sense of my life is sweet!
     though I know that the end is nigh:
   For the ruin and rain of winter will shortly come,
   The lily will lose its gold, and the chestnut-bloom
In billows of red and white on the grass will lie.

And even the light of the sun will fade at the last,
   And the leaves will fall, and the birds will hasten away,
   And I will be left in the snow of a flowerless day
To think on the glories of Spring,
     and the joys of a youth long past.

Yet be silent, my heart!
     do not count it a profitless thing,
To have seen the splendour of the sun,
     and of grass, and of flower!
To have lived and loved! for I hold
     that to love for an hour
Is better for man and for woman
     than cycles of blossoming Spring.

Oscar Wilde (1854–1900)

THE GARDEN OF EDEN

And the Lord God planted a garden eastward in Eden;
    and there he put the man whom he had formed.
And out of the ground made the Lord God to grow
    every tree that is pleasant to the sight, and good for food;
    the tree of life also in the midst of the garden,
    and the tree of knowledge of good and evil.
And a river went out of Eden to water the garden; and
    from thence it was parted, and became into four heads.

. . . And the Lord God took the man, and put him
    into the garden of Eden to dress it and to keep it.
And the Lord God commanded the man, saying,
    Of every tree of the garden thou mayest freely eat:
But of the tree of the knowledge of good and evil,
    thou shalt not eat of it: for in the day
    that thou eatest thereof thou shalt surely die.

. . . And when the woman saw that the tree was good
    for food, and that it was pleasant to the eyes, and a tree
    to be desired to make one wise, she took of the fruit
    thereof, and did eat, and gave also unto her husband
    with her; and he did eat.
And the eyes of them both were opened,
    and they knew that they were naked; and they sewed
    fig leaves together, and made themselves aprons.
And they heard the voice of the Lord God walking
    in the garden in the cool of the day: and Adam
    and his wife hid themselves from the presence
    of the Lord God amongst the trees of the garden.

... And the Lord God said, Behold, the man is become
   as one of us, to know good and evil: and now,
   lest he put forth his hand, and take also
   of the tree of life, and eat, and live for ever.
Therefore the Lord God sent him forth from the garden
   of Eden, to till the ground from whence he was taken.
So he drove out the man; and he placed at the east
   of the garden of Eden Cherubims, and a flaming sword
   which turned every way, to keep the way of the tree of life.

from Genesis, *Chapters 2 and 3*

THE LAKE ISLE OF INNISFREE

I will arise and go now, and go to Innisfree,
And a small cabin build there, of clay and wattles made;
Nine bean rows will I have there, a hive for the honey bee,
And live alone in the bee-loud glade.

And I shall have some peace there,
    for peace comes dropping slow,
Dropping from the veils of the morning
    to where the cricket sings;
There midnight's all a-glimmer, and noon a purple glow,
And evening full of the linnet's wings.

I will arise and go now, for always night and day
I hear lake water lapping with low sounds by the shore;
While I stand on the roadway, or on the pavements grey,
I hear it in the deep heart's core.

William Butler Yeats (1865–1939)

THE GLORY OF THE GARDEN

Our England is a garden that is full of stately views,
Of borders, beds and shrubberies and lawns and avenues,
With statues on the terraces and peacocks strutting by;
But the Glory of the Garden lies in more than meets the eye.

For where the old thick laurels grow along the thin red wall,
You find the tool- and potting-sheds which are the heart of all;
The cold-frames and the hot-houses, the dungpits and the tanks,
The rollers, carts and drain-pipes, with the barrows and the planks.

And there you'll see the gardeners, the men and prentice boys
Told off to do as they are bid and do it without noise:
For, except when seeds are planted and we shout to scare the birds,
The Glory of the Garden it abideth not in words.

And some can pot begonias and some can bud a rose,
And some are hardly fit to trust with anything that grows:
But they can roll and trim the lawns and sift the sand and loam,
For the Glory of the Garden occupieth all who come.

Our England is a garden, and such gardens are not made
By singing: – 'Oh how beautiful!' and sitting in the shade,
While better men than we go out and start their working lives
At grubbing weeds from gravel-paths with broken dinner-knives.

There's not a pair of legs so thin, there's not a head so thick,
There's not a hand so weak and white, nor yet a heart so sick,
But it can find some needful job that's crying to be done,
For the Glory of the Garden glorifieth everyone.

Then seek your job with thankfulness and work till further orders,
If it's only netting strawberries or killing slugs on borders;
And when your back stops aching and your hands begin to harden,
You will find yourself a partner in the Glory of the Garden.

Oh, Adam was a gardener and God who made him sees
That half a proper gardener's work is done upon his knees.
So when your work is finished you can wash your hands and pray
For the Glory of the Garden, that it may not pass away!
And the Glory of the Garden it shall never pass away!

Rudyard Kipling (1865–1936)

GARDEN, GIVERNY

Delphiniums, sweet williams,
purple gladioli,
against yellow asters, marigolds,
the whirl of sunflowers;
glimpsed pink walls against emerald shutters.

A bamboo-grove
lurks in the shadows by the lily-pond,
patient as a tiger.
Lovers kiss on a Japanese bridge
watched by the bearded phantom
from behind the willows,
sad as a blind girl in a summer garden.

Adrian Henry (1932–)

The Lover and the Beloved

I am the rose of Sharon, and the lily of the valleys.
As the lily among thorns,
   so is my love among the daughters.
As the apple tree among the trees of the wood, so is my
   beloved among the sons. I sat down under his shadow
   with great delight, and his fruit was sweet to my taste.
He brought me to the banqueting house,
   and his banner over me was love.
Stay me with flagons, comfort me with apples:
   for I am sick of love.
His left hand is under my head,
   and his right hand doth embrace me.
I charge you, O ye daughters of Jerusalem, by the roes,
   and by the hinds of the field, that ye stir not up,
   nor awake my love, till he please.
The voice of my beloved! behold, he cometh leaping
   upon the mountains, skipping upon the hills.
My beloved is like a roe or a young hart: behold,
   he standeth behind our wall, he looketh forth
   at the windows, shewing himself through the lattice.
My beloved spake, and said unto me, Rise up, my love,
   my fair one, and come away.
For, lo, the winter is past, the rain is over and gone;
The flowers appear on the earth;
   the time of the singing of birds is come,
   and the voice of the turtle is heard in our land;

PARADISI IN SOLE.
Paradisus Terrestris.
or
A Garden of all sorts of pleasant flowers which our
English ayre will permitt to be noursed vp:
with
A Kitchen garden of all manner of herbes, roots, & fruites,
for meate or sause vsed with vs,
and
An Orchard of all sorte of fruitbearing Trees
and shrubbes fit for our Land
together
With the right orderinge planting & preseruing
of them and their vses & vertues
Collected by John Parkinson
Apothecary of London.
1629

Qui veut parangonner l'artifice a Nature,
Et nos Parcs à l'Eden, indiscret il injure.

Le vas de l'elephant parle pes du ciron,
Et de l'Mispe le vol par cil du moucheron.

The fig tree putteth forth her green figs,
    and the vines with the tender grape give a good smell.
Arise, my love, my fair one, and come away.
O my dove, that art in the clefts of the rock, in the secret
    places of the stairs, let me see thy countenance,
    let me hear thy voice; for sweet is thy voice,
    and thy countenance is comely.
Take us the foxes, the little foxes,
    that spoil the vines: for our vines have tender grapes.
My beloved is mine, and I am his: he feedeth among the lilies.
Until the day break, and the shadows flee away, turn,
    my beloved, and be thou like a roe or a young hart
    upon the mountains of Bether.

from The Song of Solomon, *Chapter 2*

Kubla Khan

In Xanadu did Kubla Khan
    A stately pleasure-dome decree:
Where Alph, the sacred river, ran
Through caverns measureless to man
    Down to a sunless sea.
So twice five miles of fertile ground
With walls and towers were girdled round:
And there were gardens bright with sinuous rills
Where blossomed many an incense-bearing tree;
And here were forests ancient as the hills,
Enfolding sunny spots of greenery.

But O, that deep romantic chasm which slanted
Down the green hill athwart a cedarn cover!
A savage place! as holy and enchanted
As e'er beneath a waning moon was haunted
By woman wailing for her demon-lover!
And from this chasm, with ceaseless turmoil seething,
As if this earth in fast thick pants were breathing,
A mighty fountain momently was forced;
Amid whose swift half-intermitted burst
Huge fragments vaulted like rebounding hail,
Or chaffy grain beneath the thresher's flail:
And 'mid these dancing rocks at once and ever
It flung up momently the sacred river.
Five miles meandering with a mazy motion
Through wood and dale the sacred river ran,
Then reached the caverns measureless to man,

And sank in tumult to a lifeless ocean:
And 'mid this tumult Kubla heard from far
Ancestral voices prophesying war!

    The shadow of the dome of pleasure
        Floated midway on the waves;
    Where was heard the mingled measure
        From the fountain and the caves.
It was a miracle of rare device,
A sunny pleasure-dome with caves of ice!

    A damsel with a dulcimer
        In a vision once I saw:
    It was an Abyssinian maid,
        And on her dulcimer she played,
    Singing of Mount Abora.
    Could I revive within me,
    Her symphony and song,
To such a deep delight 'twould win me,
That with music loud and long,
I would build that dome in air,
That sunny dome! those caves of ice!
And all who heard should see them there,
And all should cry, Beware! Beware!
His flashing eyes, his floating hair!
Weave a circle round him thrice,
    And close your eyes with holy dread,
    For he on honey-dew hath fed,
And drunk the milk of Paradise.

Samuel Taylor Coleridge (1772–1834)

PAST, PRESENT,
FUTURE

FERN HILL

Now as I was young and easy under the apple boughs
About the lilting house and happy as the grass was green,
   The night above the dingle starry,
      Time let me hail and climb
   Golden in the heydays of his eyes,
And honoured among wagons I was prince of the apple towns
And once below a time I lordly had the trees and leaves
      Trail with daisies and barley
   Down the rivers of the windfall light.

And as I was green and carefree, famous among the barns
About the happy yard and singing as the farm was home,
   In the sun that is young once only,
      Time let me play and be
   Golden in the mercy of his means,
And green and golden I was huntsman and herdsman, the calves
Sang to my horn, the foxes on the hills barked clear and cold,
      And the sabbath rang slowly
   In the pebbles of the holy streams.

All the sun long it was running, it was lovely, the hay
Fields high as the house, the tunes from the chimneys, it was air
   And playing, lovely and watery
      And fire green as grass.
   And nightly under the simple stars
As I rode to sleep the owls were bearing the farm away,
All the moon long I heard, blessed among stables, the nightjars
   Flying with the ricks, and the horses
      Flashing into the dark.

And then to awake, and the farm, like a wanderer white
With the dew, come back, the cock on his shoulder: it was all
   Shining, it was Adam and maiden,
      The sky gathered again
   And the sun grew round that very day.
So it must have been after the birth of the simple light
In the first, spinning place, the spellbound horses walking warm
   Out of the whinnying green stable
      On to the fields of praise.

And honoured among foxes and pheasants by the gay house
Under the new made clouds and happy as the heart was long,
   In the sun born over and over,
      I ran my heedless ways,
   My wishes raced through the house high hay
And nothing I cared, at my sky blue trades, that time allows
In all his tuneful turning so few and such morning songs
   Before the children green and golden
      Follow him out of grace,

Nothing I cared, in the lamb white days, that time would take me
Up to the swallow thronged loft by the shadow of my hand,
   In the moon that is always rising,
      Nor that riding to sleep
   I should hear him fly with the high fields
And wake to the farm forever fled from the childless land.
Oh as I was young and easy in the mercy of his means,
      Time held me green and dying
   Though I sang in my chains like the sea.

Dylan Thomas (1914–53)

THE SOWER

I hoed and trenched and weeded,
    And took the flowers to fair:
I brought them home unheeded;
    The hue was not the wear.

So up and down I sow them
    For lads like me to find;
When I shall lie below them,
    A dead man out of mind.

Some seed the birds devour,
    And some the season mars,
But here and there will flower
    The solitary stars,

And fields will yearly bear them
    As light-leaved spring comes on,
And luckless lads will wear them
    When I am dead and gone.

       from A Shropshire Lad
    A.E. Housman (1859–1936)

A CHILD'S VISION

Under the sweet-peas I stood
And drew deep breaths. They smelt so good.
Then, with strange enchanted eyes,
I saw them change to butterflies.

Higher than the skylark sings
I saw their fluttering crimson wings
Leave their garden-trellis bare
And fly into the upper air.

Standing in an elfin trance
Through the clouds I saw them glance . . .
Then I stretched my hand up high
And touched them in the distant sky.

At once the coloured wings came back
From wandering in the Zodiac.
Under the sweet-peas I stood
And drew deep breaths. They smelt so good.

Alfred Noyes (1880–1958)

DAFFODILS

I wandered lonely as a cloud
    That floats on high o'er vales and hills,
When all at once I saw a crowd,
    A host, of golden daffodils;
Beside the lake, beneath the trees,
Fluttering and dancing in the breeze.

Continuous as the stars that shine
    And twinkle on the Milky Way,
They stretched in never-ending line
    Along the margin of a bay:
Ten thousand saw I at a glance,
Tossing their heads in sprightly dance.

The waves beside them danced; but they
    Out-did the sparkling waves in glee:
A poet could not but be gay
    In such a jocund company:
I gazed – and gazed – but little thought
What wealth the show to me had brought:

For oft, when on my couch I lie
    In vacant or in pensive mood,
They flash upon that inward eye
    Which is the bliss of solitude,
And then my heart with pleasure fills
And dances with the daffodils.

William Wordsworth (1770–1850)

STRAWBERRIES

There were never strawberries
like the ones we had
that sultry afternoon
sitting on the step
of the open french window
facing each other
your knees held in mine
the blue plates in our laps
the strawberries glistening
in the hot sunlight
we dipped them in sugar
looking at each other
not hurrying the feast
for one to come
the empty plates
laid on the stone together
with the two forks crossed
and I bent towards you
sweet in that air
in my arms
abandoned like a child
from your eager mouth
the taste of strawberries
in my memory
lean back again

let me love you
let the sun beat
on our forgetfulness
one hour of all
the heat intense
and summer lightning
on the Kilpatrick hills

let the storm wash the plates

Edwin Morgan (1920–)

I remember, I remember

I remember, I remember
The house where I was born,
The little window where the sun
Came peeping in at morn;
He never came a wink too soon
Nor brought too long a day;
But now, I often wish the night
Had borne my breath away!

I remember, I remember
The roses red and white,
The violets and the lily cups –
Those flowers made of light!
The lilacs where the robin built,
And where my brother set
The laburnum on his birthday, –
The tree is living yet!

I remember, I remember
Where I was used to swing,
And thought the air must rush as fresh
To swallows on the wing;
My spirit flew in feathers then,
That is so heavy now,
And summer pools could hardly cool
The fever on my brow!

I remember, I remember
The fir trees dark and high;
I used to think their slender tops
Were close against the sky:
It was a childish ignorance,
But now 'tis little joy
To know I'm farther off from heaven
Than when I was a boy.

Thomas Hood (1799–1845)

Cherry Blossom

Loveliest of trees, the cherry now
    Is hung with bloom along the bough,
And stands about the woodland ride
    Wearing white for Eastertide.

Now, of my threescore years and ten,
    Twenty will not come again,
And take from seventy springs a score,
    It only leaves me fifty more.

And since to look at things in bloom
    Fifty springs are little room,
About the woodlands I will go
    To see the cherry hung with snow.

from A Shropshire Lad
A.E. Housman (1859–1936)

Rosaceae

Prunus Padus
Birdcherry.

LIST OF ILLUSTRATIONS

Index of First Lines

ACKNOWLEDGMENTS

The publishers would like to thank the following for permission to include in-copyright material:

Caroline Sheldon Literary Agency for 'Palm Tree King' by John Agard from *Palm Tree King* (Pluto Press); Bloodaxe Books for 'Hydrangeas' by Moniza Alvi from *Carrying My Wife*; David Higham Associates for 'Green Man in the Garden' by Charles Causley from his *Collected Poems* (Macmillan); The Society of Authors for 'Come-Gone' from *The Complete Poems of Walter de la Mare*; The Random House Group for 'Marigolds' by Vicki Feaver from *The Handless Maiden* (Cape); The Society of Authors for 'Fairies' by Rose Fyleman; Rogers, Coleridge & White and the author for 'Garden, Giverny' by Adrian Henry from *Wish You Were Here*; The Society of Authors for 'Loveliest of Trees' and 'LXIII' from *A Shropshire Lad* by A.E. Housman; Carcanet Press for 'Strawberries' by Edwin Morgan from his *Collected Poems*; Curtis Brown Ltd for 'Bugs' by Ogden Nash; Faber & Faber and David Higham Associates for 'Early March' by Norman Nicholson from *Rock Face*; The Society of Authors for 'A Child's Vision' by Alfred Noyes; The Random House Group and Alfred A. Knopf for 'The Connoisseuse of Slugs' by Sharon Olds from *The Sign of Saturn*: Poems 1980-1987 (Secker & Warburg); Duckworth Publishers & Viking Penguin for 'One Perfect Rose' by Dorothy Parker from *The Portable Dorothy Parker*; Faber & Faber and Alfred A. Knopf, a division of Random House, Inc. for 'Mushrooms' by Sylvia Plath; Curtis Brown Group Ltd, London, on behalf of Nigel Nicolson for the extract from Vita Sackville-West's *The Garden* (Michael Joseph), copyright © Vita Sackville-West 1946; David Higham Associates and New Directions Publishing Corporation for 'Fern Hill' by Dylan Thomas from his *Collected Poems* (J.M. Dent) copyright © 1945 by The Trustees for the Copyrights of Dylan Thomas; A.P. Watt Ltd on behalf of Michael B. Yeats for 'The Lake Isle of Innisfree' by W.B. Yeats.

The publishers apologise to any copyright holders that they were not able to trace and would like to hear from them.